SELVE

by the same author

*

Marginal Land (Peterloo Poets, 1988)

Selves

M. R. PEACOCKE

For Richie
with very best wishes

Meg

PETERLOO POETS

First published in 1995
by Peterloo Poets
2 Kelly Gardens, Calstock, Cornwall PL18 9SA, U.K.

Printed in Great Britain by
Penwell Ltd, Callington, Cornwall

ACKNOWLEDGEMENTS :
Some of these poems have appeared in *The London Magazine, The Oxford Magazine, Pivot* (New York) and the *Spectator.*

"Nameless" was first published in *Neighbours,* (Peterloo Poets/BBC, 1988).

The sequence, "We're Staying at the Castlemount, Western Esplanade" was first published in *Northern Poetry 1,* (ed. Byron & Lyons, Littlewood Press, 1989).

"Goose Hymn" and "Walking to Church, 1940" were prizewinners in the Lancaster Poetry Competitions of 1989 and 1992.

"Being Weasel" won fourth prize in the National Poetry Competition, 1989.

"The Anatomy of the Horse" was commended in the Arvon Poetry Competition, 1987.

"Remembrance" won fifth prize in the Peterloo Poets Open Poetry Competition, 1987.

"Tango", from "A History of the Thé Dansant", won first prize in the Peterloo Poets Open Poetry Competition, 1994 and was shortlisted for the Forward Prize.

For my brother, Richard Rodney Bennett

Contents

Selves

It's years, Jack. What's brought you now,
half way up from the village, not even
on your own patch? The gearchange, maybe,
accomplished smoothly for once? You'd
have approved. It's you all right,
neat hand half hidden in a linked cuff,
good tweeds, brogues placed squarely.

Distances in this snowlight
are ambiguous: I'm watching the road
and seeing a lamp, and you at Bridge
gleefully making a contract;
you witnessing papers: sharp half-smile
and the lightly flourished signature,
Dorothy Vera.

There are secret compartments
to memory's box, not to be forced,
but pressure in the right place
and the springs oblige. There! Hidden
significant trifles, like you saying
Threescore and ten's enough, I'm
not driving on borrowed time.

I've scraps here of your passion
for puzzles, crosswords, codes, and all
the intricacies of constructing
your dead father's dead loved son.
So who was it I cared for?
You? Your father's fancy?
An unacknowledged part of me?

It seems you've brought a message
about our unlived selves, haunters
of the body, hungry for being.
Then tell me, Jack, what debtor self
laid itself on the line
that sultry August afternoon
and let the down train crack it?

Walking to Church, 1940

Walking to church, we stamp our shapes
on flat grey air, steel sea behind
rolled out in the same dimension,

the lanes gritty with patience, elms
ranged in memory's pop-up book
like barlines in the squareset hymns

we are shortly to sing. The squeezed
organ notes will bump like dinghies
waiting for the congregation

to shift themselves gingerly in,
but my father will steer the bass,
dominant, tonic, the known ropes.

It is warwork, like arranging
billets for evacuees, each
labelled and slotted into place.

Meanwhile the bells are swinging full
fathom through the changes, clashing
and colicky at times but sure

of a destination. So we
step briskly out between the pinched
February banks, the sun's stare

pale above us; as though the frayed
geometry of fields and towns
that passing Spitfire sees will hold

just as long as we man the pews
in time to let the crotchets march
in their fervently sober ranks,
while rage and loss stay locked in psalms.

The Anatomy of the Horse

In 1756, George Stubbs, anatomist and painter of horses, went to live in a remote Lincolnshire farmhouse with his common-law wife, Mary Spencer. Here he dissected horses and made studies for the eighteen plates of his book, *The Anatomy of the Horse*, which was published in folio in 1756.

Near derelict. Neighbours — none.
Roof sound enough to keep out weather.
Trusses and purlins, oak.
This will serve.

Tackle: bars pulleys slingdogs chains
well forged and paid for.
Good broad webbing.
Wind makes all creak like a Channel packet.

To begin at first light.

Draymen early.
Sun came up as full as an eye
and glazed and shrank.
Moon like a pan of tallow.
1st mare slung up   rigged to the life.

To record laterally   from the front   from the rear.
Graphite and red chalk   pen and ink.

All to be done from nature.

Good breeze Thursday.

new flensing knife
3 more buckets
twine
bone pit evening
ditch

Cooperage — Lincoln?
Mary — more clean rag for my face.

Preparatory drawings 3rd anatomical Table.
Fine facial nerves
Blood vessels in red

Nature at every point surpasses art.
This I surmised as a child and confirmed in Italy.

Musculus caninus   elevator of the corner of the mouth

Lips patient   drooping

Have requested sound carcasses and would pay.
Draymen tipped out a spavinned nag   galled

Rictus of laughter 'Work for a dead horse'
Musculus caninus

If certain muscles were to be disengaged, would emotion be felt?

Seat of fear?
Suffering expressed in a tubercle?
The smooth hide has not suffered.

I will look into nature for myself and consult and copy her only.

Fiction of Paradise. A stasis — a hell.
Joy without knowledge of suffering — folly.

The godlike man?

Stuff out the great veins with quills.

No distaste in my mind.
What makes the gorge rise?
A man has discipline and can study.

Demonstrate what is.

Dreamed a foal in my Mary's belly.
She unmantled herself   brown robe falling

Caul of nerves web of veins
foetus in its housing.
It wept.

Seat of the soul?

Kingcups over   cuckoos
frogs in ditches   meadowsweet   dogroses
spires of loosestrife beginning to form

Rankness and sweetness

3rd carcass.
Flare of nostril turn of ear
and how the cropped tail moves
Stars   viscous ivory

I have stamina and capacity.

5th anatomical Table.
Flesh almost away.
Jawbone   moon   halved wafer

Remember how the mares squealed and bickered under the oaks,
brushtailed foals craning for the teat.

Work till the naked eye come at the naked truth.
When I have understood, I shall paint them to the life.

Screaming of swifts   Larks pulleying up
Huzz and frenzy of messengers

I sluiced my head under the pump and put back my stained hat.

Wax to bulk out the concavities.

To reveal, not judge.

To represent those ligaments
which bind down the tendons of the muscles
to keep them in their proper places.

Thundery this evening

Fetor   My palate clogged

What is the peritoneum enclosing the heavenly bodies?

Flygod sat whinnying on the orb of my eye
Mary waked me

Obverse of love — cruelty. Taste this.

My whetstone broken

I am weary   eyes mere blebs

This muscle arising from the lateral part and ridge of the radius,
the thumb and forefinger of the horse being wanting,
is inserted into the imperfect metacarpal bone
and lost in the ligaments inserted into that bone.

My thumb and forefinger balancing pencil and red chalk
abductor policis manus   extensor longus   brevis policis manus
moving

Broad ligaments of the eyelids fending off sleep

7th a black cob trampling air
and how that swings   ears laid back
rib cage enormous
belly hoist between the cranking limbs
and how that turns

I am Jonah   Diogenes in a barrel

Mary brought bread, cheese and sweet water.
Feet set a little wide.   Apron higher.
She has reproached me not once.

Preparatory drawings 18th anatomical Table.

Summer at an end
My best knives honed almost away

Maps of flesh charts of bone

Putrid carcass
creation of God
A Barbary horse which the lion took
ferocity of God
Mary at the water trough pounding my stiffened linen
tenderness of God

Interpret nothing.
Represent not love not hate but bone.

Head of femur, lilac. Beware lilac.
Truth is as colourless as water.

I understand no more than a waggoner.

Hock   pastern   hoof   miring up sleep

Where does the life reside?

Study to engrave.

Reading the Deer

In the new plantation below the house,
young snow; and the record of deer.

Each foot drove slantwise to the brown,
cleaving over a white quill.
Here they plaited a track.
Unravelled here — three, four —
scraped away, pulled up moss,
dropped buttercup leaves, bit plantain.
Black grouse leapt up here,
primaries smacking the drift
in sharp fans; did the roe startle?
Now by the alders; the broken wall;
the ditch rank with mint. One dawdled,
stepping aside: willow twigs nipped off.
Lost now under birches and hazels
where snow has scarcely lodged,
skeining to the beck through wet clay.

A shift in air. Broad flakes begin,
filling and blurring patterned tracks of boots
that have trampled the path of the deer.

Grisedale

This is the place, high and hidden
as a glacial pool. The lane coasts
through rush and heather, down
to a seamed lap of turf that smells
of sweetgale, honey-acid.

Chapel's a cottage now. Petunias. Fuchsias.
Floundering ochre daisies. Hens.
Tarmac gives out beyond the cattle grid
where late hay's baled and stacked
like derelict chimneys.
              At Fea Fow

someone's still living. Reachey's roofs
are almost sound, the bedrooms packed
with overwintered hay. (How did they live
with such small windows? Half dark
of lamps, half dark of winter days.)

Above the bridge at East Scale
where two becks meet, the dead
lie in a little garth.
West Scale is humbled among nettles.
Round Ing's the last, the furthest fallen.

Far down by Chapel House, a bantam cock
flourishes his bravado. That thin sound
Glints against the fell. Time's up.
The dark beck shivers over stones,
nosing for the place where it must go.

Travelling Men

One, his flint eyes knapped
almost to the core, fends
lonehanded for the tribes that racket
in caverns of his brindle
tobacco beard, and captures mobs
of words in carrier bags. Force
of their opposition staggers him
in lanes and gateways.
                                    One

whose boots in their annual ellipse
bring him across my yard, holds out
a flask, and smiles. *Some taste to it
I'd like and plenty of sugar.* Once
he slept at the road end, head
on a tuft of grass, spine to warm tarmac,
wrists and ankles crossed. A pilgrimage
may take as long as it pleases.

One sells poems, costing a coffee
and cheap at the price, rhymed,
streaming across the unfolded page
in seriffed capitals. He speaks
respectfully, like a connoisseur,
of the manners of rats, who share
his appreciation of first class
newsprint, for preference *The Times.*

There is the one who is away,
hearth swept, wood stacked, bottles ranged,
binder twine noosed up.
Black bivouac of plastic
sags and bulges, breathing
a trespassing wind.
Under the beeches near the badgers' road
a presence says, Keep out.

Alien tramping kin. I know
bits of myself in them.
Once, on a swarming street, a man stood
barefoot, and asked for nothing.
I gave him coins, and he gave me
his friendly gaze, blue
as the journeying sky, brotherly.
I keep it by me where I go.

The Watcher

He knows, the old man
in the good black overcoat: where the bids
are coming from, and the bets;

whose hand's worth the spit
clapped into it; how to judge a heifer,
a tup, a dog or a lass;

when best to store, when
to sell; what's afoot in the Council rooms.
The slates of his kitchen floor

are beaten to silk
by generations of hobnails. He wears
handstitched cloth, burnished leather.

He should be buried
on a high green ridge like a chieftain, knob
of his stick in the socket

of his palm, fob watch
and Land Rover keys in place, bitches
he bred, mother and daughter,

close in by. Meanwhile
he sits in a coign of the Mart, his grin
like a bagful of ferrets.

Nameless

I do not know her name.
Clearing the trough, I found
her shadow and wore it home.
Our steps moved easily
over the broken ground,
flagstones, pineapple weed.
We paused to watch a lamb
and the first brimstone butterfly
gladdening in the sun.
   She is one and many,
my undiscerned companion;
evidence of her life
bits and pieces thrown away
or lost, like this garden fork,
roughly forged, its handle gone,
under a litter of sycamore leaf
and nettle lightly buried.
   My hands like hers have thickened,
hoping to mould time
into a good loaf;
like her I bend my back
to root out thistle and dock
and trap the rat that capers under the roof.
Jetsam on this land,
labouring to eke out the hay
through meagre February,
perhaps at best we learn
to stand and note the streak of lime
that shows where already starlings are raising a brood
in the wall badged with lichen.

The Lambs

The fields are sharp with lambs
playing at rimram, bagsy, dogger,
packdaddle, mind-yer-back, zingo,
rog-in-the-alley.

Under the chisel of rain, wind
or white March sun, their coats
are ribbed and coiled. Their split feet
stamp budprints by the stile.

Air shivers with their bawling.
Beneath the ewes, in muggy tents
of fleece, with pecking mouths
their hungers jolt and cram.

Summer must thicken, wool and flesh
grow heavy, the lambs' cries
turn habit and the echoes fall
too listless to speak back.

I took my coat. Wagons were crawling
at the lane foot, packed
with a heaving silence. The fell, empty.
The crop, taken.

Being Weasel

To be weasel: to stain grasses
with jets of musk; to thieve,
hobnob and bicker in winter sun,
hard fur packed between toes
and buckwheat pads of the foot;
to dance in bristling ellipses
intent upon a vein. Dying,
to scream in the cat's mouth twice.

The small corpse disgraced with blood
grew dull and stiffly crescent,
its almond head split wide, fixed
in the impetus of rage, its reek
on my bald huge hands.
I dug a hole, along with the dead thing
tossed in certain human perplexities
and in the kitchen set down milk.

Goose Hymn

We lub us ogre
It like we   two legi
Two blue eye
It dict us born

It warm us   dict us lib
It look us lub   feed us
goin out   comin in
Mind it mangly boot

It go unwingly
Lub it corni corni cop ya
Mind it strangly finger
it strongly anger

It frighten we
It mighty mighty alway
It might alway
might dict us die

A History of the Thé Dansant

1. FOXTROT

The briefest card my dear we are leaving
Imagine the long curve of the Blue Train
like the line of a mouth closed and smiling
and Charles in the opposite window seat
head thrown back the smoke from his cigarette
coiling and coiling There is a fellow
in the carriage with artificial legs
and a scar on his face unspeakable

My hem is in handkerchief points my head
is a gleaming oval on the fluid
stem of my spine I shall turn my shoulders
the silhouette narrow and disengaged
Imagine the endless fluted bias
of the waves I shall show my creamy back
Write to the Hôtel Blanc I am learning
a modern geometry of desire

2. SLOW FOXTROT

Lacquer bows to bleu marine,
fingerwaved, who must respond
as though she were not gratified.

Begin the formal promenade.
The sea is wrinkled like a skin
and laps the darkly pitted sand.

A liner moving Tunis-bound
sets the powdered stars aside,
jewelling the bay alone,

and creeping on and creeping on,
elegant, à la mode,
fades away from sight of land.

And don't you love the negro band?
Don't you adore the saxophone?
Your nails are painted deep as blood.

Softly flexing insteps glide
attentive to the livelong end
beneath the scalpel of the moon.

3. TANGO

Let us invent marble and five o'clock.
I'll take white, you take black.
How engagingly we rhyme
across the chequered level in the perfume
of tea and petits fours.

I shall sample the tiniest slice
of the Grand Succès on the lemon terrace,
the newly apparent moon
a delicacy cat-ice thin,
fresh as mimosa.

Your legs are dangerously long
under the palm trees at Menton,
my thighs all silk and hesitation
drawing the tango down
the polished length of the floor.

And the cellos have such slim waists
and violins are girls with flattened breasts.
Let us invent the chaise longue,
bamboo, Lapsang Souchong,
linen and panama.

You may cough and thump your stick,
but I have been up in the attic
and I have a bundle of postcards here to prove
that once we were seen to be in love
on the Riviera in nineteen twenty four.

The Picnic, after Monet

(Duet for interior voices)

Leafage of pastry a delicate bright brown.
A glazed chicken from the spit. In the country
a brown suit is appropriate, and brown boots.
Her hair is a gilded brioche.

> My coiffure sculptured, my muslin sleeves
> prisms. Let my strongest emotion
> be aquamarine and my concerns
> opalescent.

Her white dress is fanning over white linen.
It is a damask afternoon and the sky
is lightly padded — cirrus or cumulus
I forget ... A slice of the breast.

> Seasons have bruised him about the eyes.
> I incline to celadon shadows
> of parasols upon lily skin.
> Dark meat and white.

Suppose an exchange of, say, Consols
for magnolia considerations?

> His opening lips are truculent
> as geraniums.

Were we to walk the length of the avenue
(Camembert with a good Médoc)

> or saunter upon an icecream plage
> (Château Yquem)

she would be bored.

> he would be bored.

In the Museum

The light was durable and cool.
Laurus nobilis, sweet bay in pots,
marked the perspective.

In that pale gallery time had no grain.
Spring, Summer, Autumn, Winter,
goddesses of ennui

in limestone draperies unpinned, unfalling,
expounded theories of ideal form
to ghosts of bone and tissue

till she came by, twentieth century anon,
barefoot girl in a green shirt,
alive and mortal,

and melted that chill rhetoric
of an unchanging heaven
in the amen, the brief grace of being.

Découpage

(Matisse, blind)

Girl, flat as a leaf.
I looked into the blue
rectangle of an afternoon.
My scissors took my hand,
showed me she was.

Her stillness filled her.
I had not to debate
the curious question of her spine,
logic of her spaces,
crux of balance.

All was pared away
but presence. There she knelt,
fullness and emptiness the same,
encircled in one blue,
wanting nothing.

Miranda Reading her Story

She carries close her slight
weight and fragrance. *Now*, she says,
I will read it. And we prepare,
one warmth dovetailing itself
to the other. She balances head,
throat, hands. *Once ...*
A journey is in the making.

She knows the tone and summons
of magic, pressures of breath
that warn of change; interprets
blobs, wavering ovals,
threat of a zigzag line. *But
here comes snaky S.* Mysterious power
coils from her crayon, saving the day.

But in the end, she says, *they were all
vanished. It's very sad.*
She lays her paper by
and sits back, wondering. Silence fills
the print of something glimpsed
that promises no sure happy,
no ever, no after.

We're Staying at the Castlemount, Western Esplanade

1.
When I am bored I climb the attic stairs
to visit Rosie in her wooden tent.
    The skylight is a stiff blue flag. There is
the smell of varnish the smell of linen
and the damp sweetish smell of wash-hand-stands
arising from Rosie who is treadling.

Rosie is minder of a grand machine,
its figurehead a black and golden Sphinx.
    Just below the neck of the Sphinx there are
two proud cones with gilded tips. Clothed ladies
wear a single mound, right across, lower.
Rosie has only the folds of her blouse.

She tilts her bentwood chair, her eyes blue chinks.
Give us a go, please Rosie, don't be mean!
    The substance of Rosie has shaken down
into her boot which is dull black, a hoof
with metal shanks hidden under her skirt.
I think it is especially for treadling.

Be a good girl now, this won't pay the rent.
You pull this sheet and help me look for tears.
    A voice speaks from below. Rose? Rosie calls
Yes Ma'am and says in a different tone
Run along now there's a love; and I pause
just to turn back into a public child,
and march down. And that's Rosie for the day.

2.
Thinking he hears the children, Captain Kitto wakes
and shifts, and smiles; sighs in anticipation;
draws from his navy jacket chinking shells,
and waits; and sleeps again. His seamed cheeks
beneath the visor's curve are stained palm-green.
   Eyes on the canvas bulges, Annie steals
across the lawn's viridian deck, her breath
held like a captive petrel, till she peers
down at his freckled deepseasleeping head.
Under the sky's blue swell the few pale hairs
waver like seaworms. Close, her own head bowed,
she hears with glee the cowrie-clack of ancient teeth.

3.
Miss Bertram is teaching us how to paint the sea.
You need a sheet of good paper to take a wash,
a squirrel brush, few colours — blue, yellow, crimson —
and the water must be clean. Aim to work swiftly
and never, never to erase, or you'll forfeit
the quality of light, the vital quality.

The brush the sea uses is a shock of feathers,
something felted, a stick, a spar, a rag of weed.
Its colours are eelskin tarnish, rust, brown treacle.
It lays in the foreground temporary corals
of whiteling scum, and rubs out and rubs into holes
and works over and over and is never done.

4.
In sandy bathing suits, farther and farther
beyond the reach of voices.
                              In pictures,
rockpools appear like Japanese shells
flowering in a tumbler; but Annie and I
found grey barnacles, fawn jellies, black weed.

When we looked back, we saw that the undercliff
(where it is safer to play) was wearing
a huge concrete denture and holding
tiny red and blue people between its teeth.
They were jerking. We could not hear them cry.

5.
Pink's the colour of what won't last.
There are pink celluloid dollies,
pink papier mâché masks, balloons,
knickers with writing, candyfloss,
pink stick-on hearts, gobstoppers, rock —
everything struck pink and whirring
in the seaside wind.
                              Come along.
You don't want to waste your money.
You don't want to be buying those.

We sat down on the speckled sand,
stared at the waves and poked about.
Look! I've found somebody's jokebook!
You don't want to be reading that.
Are jokes pink? I'm no good at jokes
but I want to astound my friends.
Jokes are all about differences.
D'you think it's funny, the difference
between the seaside and the sea?

Mr Henry in Retirement

It was nice, the diningroom: windows upright
against the sea, white cloths as sharply cornered
as cartridge paper, metal condiment sets,
the butter perspiring in curls, the thin toast
and the convex eagle mirror with gold balls.

And one day early there was Mr Henry,
the actor, you know, in front of the mirror
like a palm tree that has burst out of its pot,
holding his trousers; violent declamations
were breaking against the rims of his stained eyes.

The nurse came. The condiments were still as mice,
linen and toast mannerly, the same grey sea
in curls beyond the glass, while Mr Henry,
the retired eagle with gold balls, grown concave
speechless and shrunken, was managed quite away.

Visitation

About the dead of August or September.
Motes settling in the airless room,
hearth still in acrid blossom
of pleated paper.
A nap of sunlight, smoothing in
through curtains, touches her, my childless aunt,
brushes her grey skin.
She lifts her arm, suppliant,

waits for the insolent rush of the god
who comes in guise of a macaw,
violently blue and yellow,
rolling the knob of his tongue like a quid
of tobacco. Grasps her. Leans to extract
the striped seed she offers in her lips.
Touching the place his antique foot has marked
she sits back laughing, flushed with worship.

And who's a good boy then? He's come
heavily home, the ginger man,
chained stomach, oiled hair,
theatrical at the door. *How's Mac?*
(Now now, be good!) And how's my girl?
watching her smile. The bird
shuts one licorice eye. She takes the ritual kiss,
unlocks the tantalus, pours whisky.

Half-Life

"From him that hath not shall be taken away even that which he hath."
— (Matthew xxv 29)

I thought I had left that house.
Today the wind has drawn me
aside for secrets, casting leaves,
straws, printed scraps. The pasty sun,
gleaming on the half-basement
of memory and through curtains
too scant to close, guides
narrowly down the stone steps
depressed like truckle beds.

Here are the mousebacks of moss in the wall.
Here is the door, brown, and the oldish
smell that wanders through. Here are the shoes
the lumpy tops of feet the dangle
of skirt the apron the hidden flesh
mounding it slack as unproved dough
the sour hands and elbows angled
to fend off some alarm. Last,
the thumb print of a face.

A wicker chair, unburdened, creaks and cries.
What can the drab in heart
inherit? Here is the child
who tweaked and teased and was gleeful
and ashamed and offered a share
of cardboard treasures,
but that one could not muster even
the colour of her eyes.
The nothing she had is taken away.

Remembrance

The Padre ministers to stumps of men.
At night the dreams come. God coughs
outside the tent, whinnies like a mule,
trails puttees of bloody bandages
and one day defects. *I am brought*
into so great trouble and misery
that I go mourning all the day long.

Three broad parishes, a small flock.
A fircone once, plumb between the eyes,
caused him to scream; a paper dart
caused a dark stain to spread.
— My text is from Isaiah
chapter fortyfive verse fifteen. *Verily*
thou art a god that hidest thyself.

Dear children this cold November morning
and some of you I know are too young
yet, remember, many are called
but few chosen. Ponder Jeremiah:
The harvest is past, the summer is ended
and we are not saved. Verily
thou art a god that hidest thyself.

At the font, at the altar, he saw his face
quake in the eye of water the eye of wine.
Gave himself up. Tidied the musty hymnals,
hung up his alb, snipped off his ribbons,
at the vestry door courtmartialled himself
and fired the shot. Jackdaws in outrage
circled the tower a full two minutes.

November Journal

Allfalldown day. Rain in the boroughs.
To London to watch old upright men
march in the posture of survival.
Before we were born, they were kitted
in homespun woollen, iron and leather,
buckskin and scarlet.

Images of those days show us youths
with simple foreheads. The custom was
to pause — whole cities halted — to trap
the echo of deaths they were used to,
but where the bolt stuns home, memory
is a crazed windscreen.

Quite soon the clocks gutter and go out
and there seems no end to the parade
through avenues without horizons.
Did we mark the calendar for this,
to watch each hand pocket the same coin
or stamped bronze token?

What can they buy in this grey market?
Obol, penny, any currency
will serve for stowing under the tongue
like a painkiller. When they arrive
at the narrow channel, it will pay
for the ferry home.

Shots of the Excavation

A young man, rueful, fingering out
a little clay. Smoothing. Assessing.
(Damaged, you see. A hole here, one there.)
Weighing between palm and palm. Looks down.
More spread in the trench, common objects
to be turned up almost anywhere.
Only of sentimental value.

A rag. A button. Yellowish sticks.
Poor unlit turnip lanterns. This one
died with his mouth wide open. Sort them
best we can into boxes. Husbands?
Fathers? Uncles? All sons, for certain,
deserving proper ceremonial
this time. Candles. Processions. Music.

A woman's face among locked faces
struggles, opens itself, weeps out words.
She is happy, a voice subtitles,
for seeing once more her brother's bones.
       Heeled in, down at the nursery garden,
lost-label roses going dirt cheap,
parched past hope. We tried, but not one took.

Comet

Plates deftly taken. Oranges
on a coarse cloth. A glass of amber tea.
Room-darkness stained with lamps, voices,
ghosts of smoke. *It's time, I think.*
Shall we go out?
              All Anatolia
lay like a blackened coin. Night
sealed the horizon, airless,
a cask inverted. Silence hissed.
One by one, emergent stars
pricked our eyes.
              Look! There!
A pale disc gliding.
A fruit fuzzy with silver. Spilled light
soaking and spreading.

Sooner than we might, we turned
to the human fug and welter
that shields us from ourselves.
High above hearing, thin, the wail
of lives perpetually departing.

Towards an Elegy

Walked as far as the bridge. Looked down.
Water deformed and formed, made anagrams
of my head. It's her birthday. How many years?

We lived upside down, slung by the knees
from railings, dangling from parapets of lies,
bounced in the hay, kept slow worms in our pockets,
sang mock opera, shrieked.

She taught me to spit.
She kept a white stallion in her bedroom
and galloped him up Shortwood Lane,
Primrose Valley, over the fivebarred gate
(effortless, responsive) and home
fresh after miles in the daisy moon.
She sampled her father's gin.

What shall we eat? Let's make a den
Let's make a fire Rub two sticks together
Snare a rabbit Boil it up in a tin
Let's get under the strawberry net
Crabapples Chestnuts Rosehips Blackberries Corn
I'll pinch some port.

'Schools awful your not aloud just not aloud.
'I only want to be a kennel maid
'so what's the point. See you in the hols P S
'I ran away to join the circus. The bloke said
'come back when your older he put me on a bus.'

Somebody's wedding. Fag in one hand
glass in the other. Huge sparkly frock.
"God you haven't changed a bit! Come and meet
George." She had the same laugh.

Her corner in the bar. Her usual order.
Her absence lengthening into afternoon.
They found her behind the kitchen door
headlong among the empties. That's what I heard.

Remembering her, I chose a flat, narrow,
perfect stone, and flicked it ducks and drakes.
It is spinning in brilliant hops towards
the place where light makes honeycomb
under the bank, and minnows
flicker and bask, finnicking unperturbed.

Thinking of Jean Muir

To smile is to disclose
briefly some fraction of the skull's
potential articulation,
manipulating its twenty two parts.

The wind through a motley
of grasses. At her slight passage
coarse acolytes divide. Could she
have been thrust mewling onto a smeared sheet?

When did she first aspire
to such nicety and rigour,
her being as a ritual art?
Might she ever have appeared smudged, inky?

A length of blackblue crepe
acknowledges the scapula,
pauses at the hip, moves downward
as a dry rain. Could she have wept, or bled?

Have woken dishevelled?
Imagination presents her
in monochrome; hankers grossly
for the affront of a chipped nail.

How many dimensions,
Madam, has death? She turns, she glides
from the hack and botch of living,
shadow on the bias of a white room.

— *Jean Muir, dress designer, died 1995.*

The Daughter

Bluebottle noon. A kiln of houses
off Huntingdon Way. Delphinium
sheaved up neat with string. Roses
limp at the door.
She is dressed in gingham
by the window in a wisp of air.

Tissues of pale meat. Brown tea.
Uncles are fumbling in their pockets
for crumpled ceremonies of money.
Monuments of thick white bread.
The mother stoops and pats
drops from the calm forehead.

Mirage of a black limousine
crosses the raw estate and sighs
to the kerb of the afternoon,
bears her away as cool as wax,
her mouse hands tucked in lilies,
child in her box.

After a Dream

I was left all day in the lurch of dreaming
like falling to the black of an eye.
No image. Something was fast on me
like a hand on the gunwale, or that thing
humped and hairless that spindled
in the mill leat when I was green.

The moon is up, mottled and in decline.
In these few hours I have learned to be old,
known myself porous, webby, brittle, acid,
Demeter searching the lodged corn
for a daughter raped and crowned, already
bride of an absolute king.

To a Friend in America

In separate continents
we are moving towards our dusk,
the ocean between us a ford
among trees, not too deep to wade.

I know your voice, the cadence of it,
and how you would come to the door
like a sister, calling There you are! Come in!
Meanwhile send me gate songs,
passwords, lantern music,
legends of the white tailed deer
and the winter hunt of stars, mysteries
succinct and full of sap.